Down on the F...

There are so many sounds that
you can hear, you can hear, you can hear.
There are so many sounds that you can hear
down on the farm.

The rooster on the fence says,
"Cock-a-doodle-doo. Cock-a-doodle-doo.
Cock-a-doodle-doo."

The rooster on the fence says, "Cock-a-doodle-doo!" down on the farm.

Cock-a-doodle-doo!

The cow in the field says,
"Moo, moo, moo. Moo, moo, moo.
Moo, moo, moo."

The cow in the field says,
"Moo, moo, moo!" down on the farm.

The pig in the pen says,
"Oink, oink, oink. Oink, oink, oink.
Oink, oink, oink."

Oink!

The pig in the pen says,
"Oink, oink, oink!" down on the farm.

The dog on the porch says,
"Woof, woof, woof. Woof, woof, woof.
Woof, woof, woof."

The dog on the porch says,
"Woof, woof, woof!" down on the farm.

The horse in the barn says,
"Hee, hee, hee. Hee, hee, hee.
Hee, hee, hee."

The horse in the barn says,
"Hee, hee, hee!" down on the farm.

The turkey in the straw says,
"Gobble, gobble, gobble.
Gobble, gobble, gobble.
Gobble, gobble, gobble."

The turkey in the straw says, "Gobble, gobble, gobble!" down on the farm.

The donkey by the wagon says,
"Hee-hee-haw. Hee-hee-haw.
Hee-hee-haw."

Hee-hee-haw!

The donkey by the wagon says,
"Hee-hee-haw!"
down on the farm.

The people on the farm say,
"How do you do? How do you do?
How do you do?"

How do you do?

The people on the farm say,
"How do you do?"
down on the farm.

Down on the farm!